Meet
ELEANOR ROOSEVELT

by Carolyn Clark

Harcourt

Orlando Boston Dallas Chicago San Diego

Visit *The Learning Site!*

www.harcourtschool.com

If you had met Eleanor Roosevelt when she was a little girl, you probably never would have guessed that she would become one of the best-known and most outspoken women of her time. She was shy and very serious. Her mother called her "Granny," making fun of her solemn, timid ways.

Eleanor was born on October 11, 1884, in New York City, the oldest child of Anna Rebecca Hall Roosevelt and Elliot Roosevelt. Anna and Elliot came from very wealthy families. They received plenty of money from their families, so they didn't have to work to make a living. Instead, they liked to have fun.

Eleanor at age three

Teddy Roosevelt

Eleanor's parents enjoyed going to parties and traveling. Elliot liked to go on adventures and hunt wild animals in the jungle. Before he married Anna, he gave her a tiger claw necklace made from a tiger he had killed on a trip to India.

The Roosevelts owned houses in the city and in the country. If they grew tired of the houses they owned, there were always plenty of relatives to visit. The Roosevelts' most famous relative was Elliot's brother Theodore, or "Teddy," who became President of the United States in 1901. Can you imagine going to visit him at the White House?

Eleanor

Elliot Roosevelt and his children

Although money was not a problem, there was a great deal of sadness in Eleanor's childhood. She adored her father and didn't want to disappoint him. Elliot loved his daughter, but he often thought she was scared too easily. Eleanor was starstruck by her beautiful, elegant mother. Anna expected her children to be miniatures of herself. Eleanor felt she could never live up to her mother's expectations.

Eleanor's mother died in 1892, when Eleanor was eight years old. Elliot, Jr., one of her two younger brothers, died in 1893. Eleanor's father died in 1894. By age ten, Eleanor had no parents.

Eleanor and her younger brother went to live with their grandmother, Valentine Hall. Her grandmother lived in a large house in the country. Eleanor studied academic subjects with a tutor. She also took piano and dancing lessons.

Grandmother Hall was very strict. When Eleanor was in her early teens, she still had to wear dresses like the ones little girls wore. Grandmother made her wear a heavy brace on her back. She also made her practice walking with a stick across her shoulders. Her grandmother thought the brace and the stick would help Eleanor's posture. Eleanor's cousin Corinne Robinson later wrote that while the rest of the family was playful, "Eleanor was just sad."

Eleanor at her grandmother's country home

Eleanor's life took a turn for the better when she was fifteen. Grandmother Hall sent her to Allenswood, a school for wealthy girls near London, England. Allenswood had only thirty-five students. Mademoiselle Marie Souvestre, known to the girls as "Sou," was the head of the school. She was from France and was about seventy years old when Eleanor arrived at Allenswood. Like Grandmother Hall, Sou was strict, but hers was a different kind of strictness. Sou insisted that the girls at Allenswood learn to think for themselves. For some of the girls this was difficult. Eleanor, however, loved being there.

Eleanor and schoolmates at the Allenswood School

Mademoiselle Marie Souvestre

When Sou assigned a paper, she expected the girls to think carefully and to write their own ideas. If she found that someone had just written what she had said in class, she threw the paper away and made the student start again.

One thing that Sou liked about Eleanor right away was that she spoke French. Sou also saw that Eleanor was kind and very intelligent. She took a motherly interest in Eleanor and had long conversations with her outside of class. She encouraged Eleanor to spend her allowance on nice clothes that made her feel pretty.

For the first time, Eleanor felt proud of herself and her own unique talents. She was happy, and it showed. Now she walked tall, showing her full 6-foot height. Years later, Eleanor would say, "I felt that I was starting a new life, free from all my former sins and traditions . . . this was the first time in my life that all my fears left me."

In 1901, when Eleanor was sixteen, Sou invited her to travel to Italy and France with her during a school break. Sou had Eleanor make the plans, buy the tickets, and pack for them both. She thought this would build Eleanor's confidence.

Eleanor and Sou stayed in small hotels, ate in local restaurants, and met many artists and writers. Sou enjoyed doing things on the spur of the moment. On one evening train ride, Sou decided that they should grab their luggage and get off the train in the middle of the trip. She wanted to take a brisk moonlight walk on an Italian beach. In Florence, Italy, Sou encouraged Eleanor to go sightseeing by herself for the very first time. Eleanor was delighted to be treated as an adult. She wrote, "Sixteen years old, keener than I have probably ever been and more alive to beauty, I sallied forth to see Florence alone." Can you imagine how excited she must have been?

The Eiffel Tower in Paris

Eleanor had a wonderful time on her vacation. She marveled at the things she saw and called the trip a "revelation." A revelation is a kind of discovery. Eleanor discovered that she could do things for herself.

When Eleanor returned to school, her spirits headed for even higher elevations. She now made friends easily and surprised herself by earning a place on the top hockey team. She later said that was one of the proudest moments of her life.

Eleanor's last year at school was her cousin Corinne's first year. Corinne, who had once felt sorry for Eleanor, wrote, "When I arrived, she was 'everything' at the school. She was beloved by everybody."

Corinne was especially impressed by how the younger girls at Allenswood looked up to Eleanor. They liked to bring her gifts. Corinne said, "Eleanor's room every Saturday would be filled with flowers because she was so admired."

Eleanor spent three years at Allenswood. She called those years "the happiest of my life." She hoped to stay for a fourth year, but Grandmother Hall insisted that she return to New York to make her debut into society. That was something wealthy young women did to show that they had become adults. After her debut, a woman was ready to find someone she would like to marry.

Eleanor never forgot Sou. Eleanor believed that what she had learned at Allenswood helped her to accomplish many things later in life. Sou did not forget Eleanor, either. She wrote to Grandmother Hall, saying that Eleanor had "the warmest heart I have ever encountered."

In the summer of 1902, Eleanor happened to see her distant cousin Franklin Roosevelt on a train. They enjoyed chatting with each other. They soon began dating and were married on March 17, 1905. The President of the United States, Eleanor's Uncle Teddy, walked the bride down the aisle.

Eleanor and Franklin

Eleanor Roosevelt in 1928

From the time Eleanor married Franklin, she was constantly busy. Eleanor and Franklin's daughter Anna was born in 1906. In the next ten years, Eleanor had five more children. She was a volunteer during World War I and helped Franklin with his political career.

In 1921, Franklin came down with polio, a disease that could not be prevented at that time. He lost the use of his legs. Eleanor helped take care of him while he was recovering. She also kept his political career alive. She volunteered for the Democratic Party, doing everything from mailing letters to making speeches. It was sometimes very difficult for her to do so many different things, but she kept working.

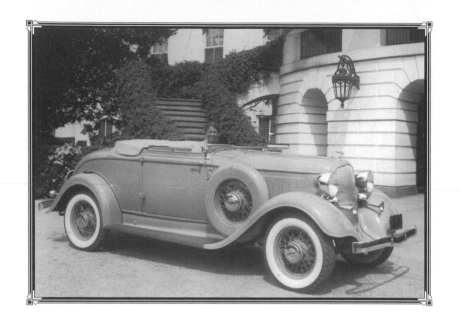

By 1928, Franklin was ready for a comeback. He was elected governor of New York. In 1932, he became President of the United States. In her practical, no-nonsense way, Eleanor told reporters, "There isn't going to be any First Lady. There is just going to be plain, ordinary Mrs. Roosevelt. And that's all." She meant she wanted people to respect her for her own accomplishments. She did not want them to think she was important just because she was the President's wife.

Mrs. Roosevelt was not ordinary, however. She wrote a daily newspaper column and earned more money from her writing than Franklin did as President. She wouldn't ride in a limousine. She drove her own car.

Eleanor was the first First Lady to fly, and she flew many thousands of miles. She did tasks that her husband could not do because he could not walk. She visited homeless people during the Great Depression and thought of ways the government could help them. In World War II, Eleanor visited soldiers in war-torn areas of England and the South Pacific. Some people even wondered if she wanted to be President someday. She said that while she was not interested, she thought that many other women were worthy. She added, "But at this time, no woman can obtain and hold the support necessary for election."

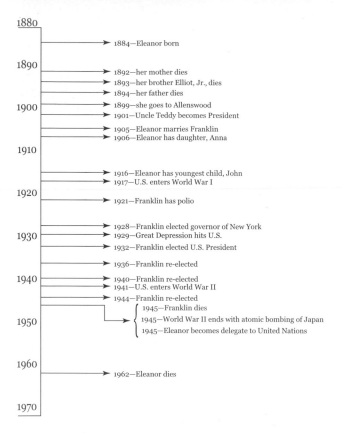

1880

1884—Eleanor born

1890

1892—her mother dies
1893—her brother Elliot, Jr., dies
1894—her father dies

1900

1899—she goes to Allenswood
1901—Uncle Teddy becomes President

1905—Eleanor marries Franklin
1906—Eleanor has daughter, Anna

1910

1916—Eleanor has youngest child, John
1917—U.S. enters World War I

1920

1921—Franklin has polio

1928—Franklin elected governor of New York
1929—Great Depression hits U.S.

1930

1932—Franklin elected U.S. President

1936—Franklin re-elected

1940

1940—Franklin re-elected
1941—U.S. enters World War II
1944—Franklin re-elected

1945—Franklin dies
1945—World War II ends with atomic bombing of Japan
1945—Eleanor becomes delegate to United Nations

1950

1960

1962—Eleanor dies

1970

Franklin's death in April 1945 didn't stop Eleanor. She worked for the United Nations and helped write the UN's Declaration on Human Rights. This declaration lists rights that people all over the world should have. She traveled the world until her death in 1962.

Eleanor Roosevelt, once a shy, timid little girl, overcame her fears to become the "First Lady of the World." She wrote, "You gain strength, courage, and confidence by every experience in which you really stop to look fear in the face . . . You must do the thing you think you cannot do."